MW00975374

VGM'S
CAREER
PORTRAITS

SCIENCE

SCIENCE

Jane Kelsey

VGM Career Horizons
a division of *NTC Publishing Group*
Lincolnwood, Illinois USA

Photo Credits:
Pages 1, 15, 29, 43, and 71: Photo Network, Tustin, CA. Page 57:
WGN TV, Chicago.
All other photographs courtesy of the author.

Library of Congress Cataloging-in-Publication Data

Kelsey, Jane
    Science / Jane Kelsey.
       p.   cm. — (VGM's career portraits)
    Includes index.
    Summary: An introduction to careers in various scientific
    fields, with portraits of people working in biology, astronomy,
    geology, physics, meteorology, and chemistry.
    ISBN 0-8442-4377-9 (alk. paper)
      1. Science—Vocational guidance—Juvenile literature.
    2. Scientists—Biography—Juvenile literature. [1. Science—
    Vocational guidance. 2. Scientists. 3. Vocational guidance.]
    I. Title. II. Series.
    Q147.K4 1996   95-49817
    502'.3—dc20   CIP
                                                 AC

Published by VGM Career Horizons, a division of NTC Publishing Group
4255 West Touhy Avenue
Lincolnwood (Chicago), Illinois 60646-1975, U.S.A.

8 9 0 QB 9 8 7 6 5 4 3 2

Contents

The scientific mind does not so much provide the right answers as ask the right questions.

Claude Lévi-Strauss
French anthropologist

Dedication

To Rachel, Matt, Mary, and Marge whose knowledge of science inspired me.

Introduction

Science infiltrates every part of our lives. Scientific research has led to the development of computers, television, airplanes, and life-saving medicines. Scientists try to answer an infinite number of questions about the world we live in: What will the weather be? How old is the earth? What is energy? Why is there a hole in the ozone layer? They study everything from atoms to the stars! No matter what you decide to do in the future, you will probably be helped in your job by some aspect of science.

Reading this book allows you to explore different science careers. Each chapter gives you a closer look at one type of scientist. You will meet biologists, astronomers, geologists, physicists, meteorologists, and chemists. You will read their career stories and learn how they feel about their jobs. You will find out what happens on the job, the pleasures and pressures of the job, the rewards, the pay, and the perks. You will also learn what education each job requires. This book will help you discover if you have the aptitude, skills, and personality to pursue a career in science. Throughout this text you will learn about some of the pioneers in science and today's giants in science as you read their success stories.

CAREERS IN BIOLOGY

B iology is a large and diverse field offering many different career choices. Biologists study plants and animals and their relationship to their environment. They study all sizes of living things from the smallest cell to the largest whale. Because more than 1.5 million different species inhabit the earth, there is much to study! With the help of biologists, a cure for polio has been found and the life expectancy of a newborn infant has almost doubled in the past 100 years. Biologists have many career options. They can do research, become technicians, or even teach!

What it's like to be a biologist

As a biologist you will probably specialize in one of the three main divisions of biology: botany, zoology, and microbiology. Botanists study plants, while zoologists study animals. Microbiology is the study of bacteria, fungi, and other microscopic organisms. Biologists generally work regular hours in offices or laboratories. However, depending on your area of specialization, you may spend some of your time outdoors doing research, possibly in remote spots.

Let's find out what happens on the job

You may be working alone or as part of a team. The type of work and where you do it as a research biologist depends on your area of specialization. Cytologists study the cells of animals and plants. They spend a great deal of their time in the laboratory. Ecologists, who study organisms and their relationship with the environment, do some of their research outside. A marine biologist studies organisms in the sea. If you become a marine biologist, you could do some of your research on a ship in the ocean or even in a bathysphere. As a biologist, you also can teach. Many biologists split their time between teaching and doing research. If you become a biology technician, you will spend much of your time assisting others. You may operate equipment or supervise test results.

The pleasures and pressures of the job

A career in biology can be very rewarding because you know that your research is helping to improve life for everyone on this planet. Some areas of biology such as plant taxonomy—the study and classification of plants—will allow you to travel and work outside while conducting research. This may require strenuous physical activity. Other areas of biology will require you to spend most of your time working in a laboratory. If you are working in a laboratory, you may be in a very competitive and pressure-filled environment. For example, the company you work for will need accurate results, and newly discovered products will have to be tested quickly and carefully. Working in a laboratory will generally not expose you to any hazardous or unsafe materials. However, some research projects might require you to work with toxic substances. While working on those projects, you will have to follow strict safety procedures.

The rewards, the pay, and the perks

Biology is a rapidly growing field where careers are fairly recession proof. Most biologists are employed in agriculture or on long-term research projects, which protect them from economic fluctuations. The average beginning salary for a biologist working in private industry is

$21,850. The average salary for all biologists is between $26,000 and $47,000. Salaries tend to be higher for biologists with more education and experience. If you earn a master's degree or a Ph.D., you will probably earn more and have a greater number of job opportunities than with just a bachelor's degree.

Getting started

For a career in biology you will need a solid background in math and science. It is a good idea to take as many of these classes as you can in high school—even earlier, if possible. A biologist needs to have a background in both physics and chemistry as well as biology. English classes are also necessary because as a biologist you will need to communicate your findings clearly. Computer expertise is absolutely essential for most research projects as well as almost every other aspect of biology.

Climbing the career ladder

A career in biology offers many opportunities for advancement, but these opportunities are tied to your level of education. With a bachelor's degree, you will be able to get an introductory-level job, work as a research assistant, or become a high school teacher. A master's degree will allow you to do applied research. It will also enable you to get a job in management, sales, or service. A Ph.D. will allow you to teach at the college level and do independent research. As you gain experience, you will be able to move into management and administration.

Do you like animals? Do you have a pet? Have you ever planted anything, or raised a garden? To become a biologist you must like to work with and have an interest in either plants or animals. If you are naturally curious and inquisitive, a career in science might be right for you. However, you will also need patience, because it may take years to get results from your research.

Biology is a very large field with many different areas of specialization. You may find that you like one area of biology, such as the study of plants, and dislike another.

Now decide if being a biologist is right for you

To become a biologist you will need to get a college degree. But you can do many things that will give you experience in and knowledge about the field of biology before you ever get into college. Gaining knowledge about biology could simply mean talking to the biology teachers at your school or participating in field trips to farms or aquariums. You could join your local 4-H club and do a biology-related project, volunteer in a hospital or find a part-time or summer job in a laboratory. There are also Student Science Training Programs (SSTP) that allow high school students to do research.

Things you can do to get a head start

Let's Meet...

Michael Ollman
Biologist

Michael spends most of his time in the laboratory doing independent research in a field that he finds fascinating.

Have you always dreamed of a career in science?

No. Although I enjoyed most of my science classes in high school and college, it was not until late in my college years that I chose to pursue a career in science.

Did you need any special schooling or training?

Considerable training is required for a career in science. Technicians usually have a bachelor's or master's degree in a scientific discipline. Research director positions require a Ph.D. or M.D. and several years of postdoctoral experience.

Describe a typical day at work.

A scientific career demands both intellectual and technical skills. An average day includes a few hours of planning experiments, analyzing data, and keeping up with the latest published research. Most of the day, however, is devoted to physical tasks involved in running experiments.

What special skills do you need to be a good scientist?

Patience, persistence, curiosity, and an ability to critically analyze assumptions and conclusions are the qualities that are most helpful.

What do you like most about your job?

The best part of my job is that I get to do independent work and make discoveries in a fascinating field.

Is there a lot of competition for jobs in scientific research?

The market for jobs in scientific research is extremely competitive. A limited number of companies and institutions support advanced research so the number of available jobs is very small.

Describe your work environment.

The work environment in scientific research is unique. Several researchers work independently in a large room, each assigned a small desk and work space. The atmosphere is very informal, and the amount of interaction depends on the personalities of your coworkers.

What is the most difficult part of your job?

Dealing with the slow pace at which progress is made in scientific research. A failed experiment can cost several days or weeks of work. Success comes in small steps, and it can be exhausting and demoralizing during the periods when little progress is made.

Michael's Daily Diary

9:00–10:00   Attend journal club, a weekly informal discussion of recent scientific publications.

10:00–11:00   Clean and assemble apparatus for running a polyacrylamide gel (a method for separating proteins based on their size). Make solutions and pour the bottom part of the gel. Discuss previous day's results with research director.

11:00–12:00   Use the sterile hood in the tissue culture room and the cold room to set up for the experiment. Pour the top part of the gel.

12:00–1:00   Grab a quick lunch and check e-mail.

1:00–5:00   Now the day gets very busy.... Analyze the 40 fractions from the protein sample. Conduct experiments that require dull, repetitive tasks such as making and mixing different solutions and samples from each of the 40 fractions, along with lots of time on the computer to turn the data into graphs that allow him to interpret the results.

5:00–6:00   Take a short break to grab a snack and chat with coworkers.

6:00–7:00   Load the protein onto the gel and apply the electric field, which will run overnight to separate the proteins.

Let's Meet...

Jennifer Hill
Biomedical Engineer

Jennifer combined a career in biology with engineering. She designs and builds prototypes for doctors to use when treating their patients.

What first attracted you to a career in biomedical engineering?

During a high school computer class, I saw a film on biomedical engineering. Electrical and mechanical engineers were working with physicians to help paraplegics walk again. I was very interested in the technology and in helping people.

How did you know you would enjoy working as a biomedical engineer?

Well, I knew that I was fascinated by the medical field, the technological aspects in particular. I also knew that I liked to problem solve and design, both are big parts of biomedical engineering.

Tell me how you got started in biomedical engineering.

While in college, I spoke with some of the professors in the field and was able to get a summer job as an engineering technician working on various medical projects. After college, I worked as a physical therapy assistant while looking for an engineering job. One of my patients helped set up an interview with the medical company for which I eventually worked.

Do you like to work alone or as part of a team?

On the whole, I am very much a team player and enjoy working with others. There are times when I need to work alone, mostly when designing or trying to work through a difficult problem for the first time.

Describe one of your happiest moments on the job.

I had worked several months designing and building prototypes for doctors to use in helping patients with vascular problems in their brains. My final prototype worked and helped fix the patients' problems.

What is the most difficult part of your job?

Biomedical engineering provides quite a bit of an intellectual challenge, not to mention creative challenges. These challenges, along with working as part of a team, are great, but there is a lack of working directly with and for people.

What is your next career move likely to be?

Though I love biomedical engineering, I miss working with people on a daily basis. Engineering did not provide me with enough "care giving." I am now pursuing medicine, where I can combine my interest in technology with the need to care for patients.

Jennifer's First Day on the Job

When Jennifer found out that she had gotten the job, her first reaction was one of excitement, enthusiasm, and relief! As her first day approached, she began feeling apprehensive and anxious. What was she getting into? A bachelor of science degree in engineering was a necessity for the job (or at least to get the job), but most of the specialized training was to take place on the job. Her under-graduate training in engineering had given her the groundwork needed for the thought process she would use in the work. The fundamentals of particular engineering areas she had learned were integrated within her biomedical engineering job.

On the first day of the job, she was excited and overwhelmed. Jennifer sat in her office and read as much about the projects going on as she could. She acquainted herself with the people in the department, her office mate in particular. He and Jennifer had lunch that day, and he helped her realize that she would have time to learn the things she needed to know!

Success Stories

Francis Crick and James Watson

In 1962, Francis Crick and James Watson won the Nobel Prize for physiology and medicine. The two biologists had discovered and built a model of the molecular structure of deoxyribonucleic acid (DNA). Their model of DNA is known as the Watson-Crick model. They determined that DNA formed a double helix, which resembles a ladder twisted to form a spiral. DNA contains the genetic material that is passed from one generation to the next. Both Watson and Crick went on to study and try to break the genetic code. Watson and Crick's work with DNA allowed for many advancements in the fields of biology, biochemistry, and genetics.

Florence Sabin

Florence Sabin was the first woman to be elected into the National Academy of Sciences. Sabin was born in 1871 and graduated from Johns Hopkins Medical School in 1900; a university at which she later became a professor. Sabin was involved in research in human embryology. She discovered that buds on the veins of an embryo developed into blood cells and the lymphatic system. Sabin was also concerned about public health.

Find Out More

You and a career in biology

Take the following quiz to see whether a career in biology is right for you:

- Do you like plants and/or animals?
- Do you like to work outdoors?
- Would you mind spending long periods working in a laboratory?
- Do you like to travel?
- Do you work well in groups?
- Can you work well independently?
- Do you have the ability to concentrate and pay close attention to detail?
- Have you taken and enjoyed science classes offered by your school?
- Do you work well under pressure?
- Can you communicate effectively both orally and in writing?
- Are you able to work for long periods on one project?
- Are you curious and inquisitive?
- Have you ever grown a plant or taken care of an animal?

- Are you worried about the environment?

- Do you wonder about the relationship among plants, animals, and the environment?

If you answered "yes" to most of these questions, you probably possess the skills and qualities necessary to become a successful biologist.

Find out more about being a biologist

For more information about a career in the biological sciences, you may want to contact one of the following sources:

American Institute of Biological
    Sciences
730 11th Street, NW
Washington, DC 20001

American Society for Microbiology
Office of Education and Training–
    Career Information
1325 Massachusetts Avenue, NW
Washington, DC 20005

American Physiological Society
9650 Rockville Pike
Bethesda, MD 20814-3991

CAREERS IN ASTRONOMY

I magine living in space with the earth spread out beneath you, traveling from one planet to the next, gathering information about space wherever you go. With advancements in technology and science, this could describe one of the future jobs available to astronomers.

From the beginning of time, people have looked up at the stars and developed theories about how the celestial bodies were formed. Today, astronomers are still trying to figure out the sky's mysteries, and they will continue this search in the future.

What it's like to be an astronomer

Astronomy is the study of the universe and its celestial bodies. As an astronomer you would be learning more about the sun, moon, stars, planets, and galaxies. You would use special equipment to calculate the position of stars, the orbits of comets, and the structure of planets. Unlike other sciences, astronomers cannot bring what they are studying into a laboratory. Instead, astronomers must rely on the information they gather from telescopes, satellites, and supercomputers for their research. Astronomers tend to specialize in one area of their field. For example, you could specialize in celestial mechanics and devote all of your research to the study of the motion of solar objects.

Let's find out what happens on the job

It is nighttime and the stars are shining brightly. You, as an astronomer, are working at an observatory gathering information about the celestial bodies. However, you will spend only a few nights in an observatory each month, and maybe only 2 to 3 weeks total each year. The rest of your time will be spent analyzing large quantities of data from your observations and from other observatories and satellites, and writing scientific papers or reports on your findings. If you are a theoretical astrophysicist, you may not even use a telescope but rely solely on a supercomputer.

The pleasures and pressures of the job

Astronomy can be a very exciting science. In the past decade many new discoveries and observations have been made. Astronomers watched a comet collide with a planet and saw solar systems form! These same astronomers probably worked at night and in remote areas. Most research observatories are in places where the air is clean and the skies are clear, not in cities.

The rewards, the pay, and the perks

Most astronomers work at universities, splitting their time between research and teaching. Not only are they adding to the information available about space, but they are able to pass it on directly to their students. The average salary range for astronomers working at a university is $25,000 to $60,000 for 9 months. These salaries can be augmented with summer work or consulting. The salary range for astronomers employed by the government is about the same. Further education is rewarded. Astronomers who have a Ph.D. earn more than those who stopped their education after receiving a bachelor's degree.

Getting started

The classes you take in high school are important in preparing for a science career. If you want to become an astronomer, you should choose as many math and physics courses as possible. Other sciences should also be studied. Plus you need to take courses to gain computer expertise and oral and written communication skills. In college you will continue studying math and physics. It is not unusual for an astronomer to major in physics and then go on for a graduate degree in astronomy. Graduate study is required for most jobs in astronomy. Competition is keen so you will need to have excellent grades and a strong background in physics to be admitted to a graduate school.

Climbing the career ladder

As in biology and the other sciences, advancement in astronomy depends on your level of education. If you earn a bachelor's degree, you will be able to work as a research assistant or in a planetarium running a science show. With a doctorate, you will be qualified to teach at a university and to do research. The majority of astronomers work at universities and colleges. At a university you would be able to advance from an instructor to an assistant professor and eventually to a professor. If you work for the government or for a private company, advancement will depend on your experience and ability.

Now decide if being an astronomer is right for you

Do you enjoy looking at the stars? Are you good at observation? You will need good analytical skills to become an astronomer. Astronomers rely on information gathered from observations, satellites, and computers for their research. If you like to do more hands-on research, astronomy may not be the best career choice in science for you. Astronomy is a science devoted to discovery and to increasing our knowledge of the universe. If you are a logical thinker, patient, have a good imagination, and are able to concentrate for long periods of time, astronomy could be the right career choice for you.

Things you can do to get a head start

There are many ways to learn about astronomy outside of the classroom. If you would like experience using telescopes, join a local astronomy club. There are many amateur astronomy clubs across the United States. As a member of one of these clubs, you can practice making observations or even learn how to build your own telescope. You can also volunteer at a planetarium, observatory, or local science museum. As a volunteer you might even be able to assist an astronomer in research. While you are in high school or college, consider getting a summer internship that allows you to study astronomy. Many opportunities are available for young people.

Let's Meet...

Geoffrey Marcy
Astronomer

Geoffrey is a professor of astronomy and physics. He splits his time between teaching classes at San Francisco State University and doing research.

What first attracted you to a career in astronomy?

I was first drawn to astronomy when I was 14 years old. My parents bought me a small telescope, and I used to stay up late at night watching the moons orbit other planets. I would draw sketches of the moons night after night, trying to figure out how long it took for a moon to go around its host planet one time.

What special skills do you need to be a good university science teacher?

The most important skills are simply empathy and respect for the students. Knowing the science itself is the easy part. However, I think learning to respect students and listening thoughtfully to them is indeed a "skill" that can be improved with practice.

What do you like most about your job?

It's the chance to do research that can change our understanding of the universe. When I help discover something new, I feel that I've made a contribution to my generation.

Describe your happiest moments on the job.

My happiest moments occur when my collaborators and I have worked hard for months on a project, and the results are finally coming to full fruition. Sometimes, there is a moment during which we all realize that we have learned something about the nature of stars that no one has ever known. Sometimes that new knowledge opens entirely new vistas of understanding and puzzles about the universe and our solar system. I can't wait for the "Eureka!" moment when we discover the first planets orbiting another star, for the first time. Then we will know for sure that Earth is not the only habitable oasis within the dark, cold universe.

How much schooling did you need for your job?

I needed to get my bachelor's degree and a master's degree and Ph.D. in astronomy. I also spent 2 years as a postdoctoral fellow.

How did you know you would enjoy working as an astronomer?

I thought I would enjoy astronomy as a job because the questions raised are so fascinating and the answers are so profound. I thought that as an astronomer I could continue to dream about the grandeur of the universe while being reminded at the same time of how small Earth really is.

Geoffrey's Career Path

Geoffrey always tries to prepare himself for the future by anticipating the next steps in life. For example, by working hard in his
high school classes, many opportunities were available to him
when he decided to go to college, because he had already learned
the basics. This preparation allowed him to enjoy his college
classes more. He learned more, too, because his knowledge of
basics allowed him to concentrate on the details.

For Geoffrey, anticipating the future included learning subjects
in school that were not directly related to his job as a scientist. In
both high school and college, he took several English classes on
writing composition. These courses have helped him immensely as a
scientist because he often must write papers on the science research
that he does. English courses also helped him to develop a good
vocabulary and the clarity of speech that is so important for speak-
ing in front of audiences (as he does at scientific conventions).

Let's Meet...

Nathalie Martimbeau
Astronomer

Nathalie works as an astronomy assistant at a planetarium where she is able to share her lifelong fascination with stars with people of all ages.

Tell me how you got started in astronomy.

As a child I was always looking at the stars and constellations. I would look at the Big Dipper in the summer and Orion in the winter from the doorsteps of our flat. I was fascinated by the stars out there and imagined stories about them. When I was 13 years old, my family moved from the city to the country, and I was amazed to see so many more stars compared to the number I had seen in the city. It was then that I knew that I wanted to be an astronomer. When I went to college, I joined an amateur astronomy group. I also got involved in teaching astronomy in summer camps.

What do you like about your job?

I like being with people. I like teaching them what I know about astronomy and communicating my love of astronomy. I want to demystify science and to make astronomy accessible to everyone.

What special skills do you need to be a good astronomy educator?

You need to be a good observer, have a creative mind, and be able to speak in public. Of course, knowledge of astronomy is a must. Because being an astronomer is like being a detective, you need to have an extra investigative sense.

What advice would you give young people starting out in astronomy?

There is a lot of competition for jobs in astronomy. If you really love astronomy, persevere. Get to know different people who work in astronomy, cultivate your contacts, and attend conferences to meet new people. Work with a professor as a research assistant or get a job in a planetarium as an usher, a cashier, or an intern.

Describe a typical day at work.

Every day is a little different. During the school year, a day might look like this. I'll start work at 8:30 and begin by doing some paperwork at my desk. At 9:45 I go to the planetarium theater to set up for the first school show. At 10:10 we start the walk-in music, and the ushers start seating the students. The show is over by 11:15, and I set up again for the 12:00 show. By 12:45 the show is over, and I finally get to eat lunch. In the afternoon, I will return to my desk and answer public inquiries about astronomy either by phone or by mail. I am always preparing something new—an activity or a class that I will be giving in the near future.

How Nathalie Got Her Job

Nathalie had been an intern for a year at the Morrison Planetarium when the education coordinator position became vacant. While the position was vacant, she worked part-time along with two other people to do some of the tasks that needed to be done. The new position was finally posted in October. She remembers going to the university's library on a Tuesday night to get a copy of the previous weekend's newspaper for the ad. In November, she made the top five finalists' list out of 25 other applicants. For the next step, she had to send one example of a publication in astronomy that she had written and a cassette tape of a planetarium show that she had given. At this point, she was getting nervous because it was very close to the December holidays, and she wanted to know what her future would be. At the end of January, Nathalie was asked to come in for an interview about a week later. The next Monday—on the eve of Valentine's Day—she was told that she had the job. What a valentine that was!

Success Stories

Galileo Galilei

Galileo Galilei was both an astronomer and a physicist. Born in Italy in 1564, Galileo grew up in a world that still believed the sun rotated around the earth. His discoveries in astronomy and physics led him to be called the "founder of modern experimental science." In 1609, Galileo discovered that the moon was not smooth. Using a telescope that he had built, Galileo found that the moon had a rugged, mountainous surface. Galileo believed in the Copernican theory that the earth revolved around the sun. This belief got him into trouble with the church, and in 1633 he was confined to his villa in Florence for the rest of his life.

Isaac Newton

Isaac Newton is perhaps most famous for his discovery of the law of gravity; however, this English scientist was also a great inventor. Newton was very interested in the study of light; it was this interest that prompted him to build a new type of telescope. His new telescope used a reflecting mirror rather than a combination of lenses. The result was a much smaller telescope that even allowed him to see the satellites of Jupiter. Between 1665 and 1667, Newton not only discovered the secret of gravity, he also discovered the secrets of light and color and invented calculus.

Find Out More

You and a career in astronomy

Have you ever looked up into the sky at night and wondered how the stars got there? Astronomers try to answer questions about the nature of the universe. The following is a list of questions that astronomers work with every day. Have you ever thought about these same questions?

Do you know what stars and planets are? What they are made of?

How do stars and planets form? How do they die?

Do you believe there are other life forms?

How many galaxies are there? What are the differences between galaxies?

How was the universe formed? How old is it, and when will it end?

What is a quasar? How fast do quasars move?

Why do some planets, like Jupiter, have rings around them?

What is a comet? How do comets form?

**Find out
more about
being an
astronomer**

Many magazines and organizations have useful information for people interested in astronomy. If you want to find out more about a career in astronomy or would like to join an amateur astronomy club, contact one of these sources:

Magazines

Mercury
Astronomical Society of the
    Pacific
390 Ashton Avenue
San Francisco, CA 94112

Astronomy
Kalmbach Publishing Co.
21027 Crossroads Circle
Waukesha, WI 53187

Associations

Astronomical League
Science Service Building
1719 N Street, NW
Washington, DC 20036

American Association of Variable
    Star Observers
25 Birch Street
Cambridge, MA 02138

CAREERS

IN

GEOLOGY

T he earth is constantly changing: earthquakes shake the land, volcanoes erupt, and mountains erode. Geologists study how these changes affect the earth and how they might be able to mitigate them. Geology is the study of the earth—its history, structure, and origin. Geologists search for oil, gas, minerals, and underground water; construct maps; conduct geological surveys; examine rocks and fossils; use instruments to measure earth's gravity; study earthquakes; and solve

environmental problems. The earth is a geologist's
laboratory. Its vast size gives them plenty to study.

What it's like to be a geologist

Because the earth is such a large
and complex place to study, geologists often specialize in one area of
geology. Those who are fascinated
by the ocean often become oceanog-
raphers. They will spend their time
studying and mapping the ocean
floor, learning about currents, or
investigating the chemical composition of oceans. Stratigraphers concentrate on the distribution and
arrangement of sedimentary rock
layers. Hydrologists study the circulation, distribution, and physical
properties of water. Petroleum geologists explore for oil and gas, while
seismologists interpret data from
instruments to detect earthquakes
and locate earthquake-related
faults. Environmental geologists
specialize in studying, preserving,
and cleaning up the environment.

Let's find out what happens on the job

You will most likely split your time
between doing research in the field
and working in a laboratory or your
office. As much as 3 to 6 months of
your year could be spent in the field
doing research. During this time
you'll probably be taking samples,
making maps, collecting materials,
or taking measurements. Most likely you will be working on a team
with other geologists. When you
return from the field, your time will

probably be spent in a laboratory analyzing the data you have collected. This may mean continuing studies that you began in the field or starting new studies using more sophisticated equipment. You'll also work in your office writing reports about the information you have gathered and reviewed.

The pleasures and pressures of the job

The work you do as a geologist will be both physically and intellectually demanding. When doing research in the field, you might have to travel to remote regions by helicopter or four-wheel-drive vehicle and cover large areas by foot. You will be at the mercy of the weather. And the members of your team may be the only people around. However, out in the field you will enjoy the camaraderie of working on a team and the chance to see new places. Some of your work as a geologist will be routine; however, there is always the excitement of making new discoveries.

The rewards, the pay, and the perks

Geology is a very competitive field, but the demand for geologists in environmental protection and reclamation is growing. On the other hand, jobs related to the exploration for gas and oil in the United States have been curtailed due to restrictions on potential drilling sites, low oil prices, and higher production costs. The salary range is wide and depends on where you are employed. You would make the most money in the petroleum, mining, and mineral industries, but your job will be less secure. Starting salaries for geologists range from $21,000 to $44,000. Generally, the more education and experience you have, the more you will earn.

Getting started

A college degree is necessary for a career in geology as it is for most other sciences. A broad background in the sciences is recommended to prepare you for majoring in geology in college. While in high school you should take earth science, physics, chemistry, and mathematics. English is also highly recommended. Today's geologists use very sophisticated equipment to help them with their research. Be sure that you acquire the computer expertise necessary to handle the information generated by this equipment.

Climbing the career ladder

A bachelor's degree in geology is only good enough for getting lower-level geology jobs. You'll need at least a master's degree to find jobs with good potential for advancement. With a master's degree you will be able to do research; however, with a Ph.D. you will be qualified to teach in a university or college and to get work involving basic research for federal agencies.

You will probably start your career as a research assistant or in field exploration. As you gain experience, you will be given more difficult assignments. If you are working on a research project, you could be promoted to the position of team or project leader. Eventually, you could climb the career ladder into other management and research positions, such as program manager. If you are working in a university, you can expect to advance from an instructor to professor.

Now decide if being a geologist is right for you

Besides having an interest in science, you need to have an intense desire to find out more about the earth. You also have to be comfortable in the outdoors. Take the time now to discover if you have the same traits as most geologists do:

Are you good at visualizing?

Do you have perseverance?

Are you willing to attend college and probably graduate school?

Do you have stamina?

Are you in good physical condition?

Do you work well with other people?

Do you consider yourself a creative thinker?

Can you work well independently?

Let's Meet...

Jill McCarthy
Geologist

Jill works as a research geophysicist for the United States Geological Survey and studies the faults that underlie the San Francisco Bay Area.

What first attracted you to a career in geology?

In the fourth grade I read a comic book that described how the continents had at one time all been part of a single land mass (Pangea) and had subsequently drifted apart as the Atlantic Ocean opened. This was the first time I'd heard about plate tectonics or seafloor spreading, and I was completely fascinated. A trip to Yellowstone in the seventh grade increased this interest and convinced me to take a geology class as soon as I got to college. After that I was hooked.

How did you get your job?

When I was a senior in college, a guest speaker from the U.S. Geological Survey came to talk to the Geology Department. He described the geophysical work he did in the North Pacific. I asked him how to go about getting on one of these research cruises. He replied that he gets requests for jobs all the time, and the best way to get his attention was to include

something that would make me stand out. Later that fall, I sent him a letter in which I included a small rock sample and a picture I'd taken of him and some of my classmates picking pumpkins. It worked. I got a 6-month job at the USGS, which I managed to convert into a permanent position.

Did you need any special schooling?

Yes, I needed to get a master's degree in geophysics and a Ph.D. in geology.

What do you like most about your job?

My job as a research geophysicist involves periodically designing large field programs to study faults that can't be monitored at the surface. These experiments often take up to 1 year to plan. After all that effort, it's exhilarating to see the first glimpse of the data coming off the recorder. Because my research is typically reconnaissance in nature, I am often completely surprised by the data we record. It's like diving for lost treasure—until you open the treasure chest, you're not sure what kind of riches, if any, await you.

If you could start over, would you choose a different career?

No way! I feel incredibly fortunate that for 15 years I've managed to earn a good living doing the work I love. Not only am I still doing geology, but I've managed to carve out a niche where I can study plate tectonics while at the same time working on problems relating to everyday life, such as earthquake hazards.

Jill's Study of Earthquake Faults

Jill's work is presently focused on the earthquake faults in the San Francisco Bay Area. Because she studies faults up to 20 miles below the surface, the work requires the use of remote-sensing techniques. Her equipment includes very sensitive listening devices called hydrophones (similar to microphones), which require a quiet recording environment. This is difficult to find in a congested urban environment so they do their studies in the area's marine waterways.

Jill and her colleagues recently completed a 2-week study on San Francisco Bay testing a new technique for recording these deep images. They laid a 1.5-mile-long hydrophone cable directly on the seafloor and used it to record the sound energy being reflected off of deep geologic layers in the subsurface. The experiment was very challenging because high winds and rough seas made for very dangerous operating conditions. They were rewarded, however, by incredible vistas and excellent data that may eventually help them unravel how these faults are changing with time.

Let's Meet...

David Snyder
Geologist

David has been a professional geologist for 11 years. During his career he has worked on many different research projects and won several awards for his accomplishments.

What first attracted you to a career in geology?

When I was growing up, my uncle took me on wonderful camping trips to collect rocks and fossils. It was exciting to pick up a rock that was once lava from a volcano or a fossil that was once part of a tree or dinosaur. Another experience that furthered my interest in geology was the San Fernando earthquake that struck when I was 10 years old. Our whole house shook, and there was a terrible sound of breaking glass. The freeways and many of the buildings in my neighborhood collapsed. Although I was scared, I was interested in what could cause such a large and destructive earthquake. Geology is a great way to learn about the earth while you are having fun.

Describe one of your most exciting moments on the job.

When I explore a site, one method I commonly use is downhole logging. This involves drilling a

2-foot-diameter hole in the ground and then
lowering me down into it! I have gone down
more than 200 feet to look at landslides.
This is very exciting because you have to go
underneath the landslides to see how deep
they go. It is also a very important job
because the engineers have to know what
landslides look like underground to keep the
houses they build from moving.

Describe a typical day at work.

A typical day usually starts with a staff
meeting and then involves a house inspec-
tion. My job is to determine why a house is
sliding down a hill and cracking up inside.
To do this I look at geology maps and air
photos to see what conditions caused the
landslide. Then I drill holes into the hill to
determine how deep the landslide is. This
information is then supplied to our engineers so that they can design a repair for the
house. I like this type of fieldwork because
you are always exploring and you are never
sure what you are going to find.

What is special about being a geologist?

Being a geologist allows you to read a new
language that no one else can understand.
After school, when you look around, it is
like seeing large signs and billboards with
writing on them that are invisible to everyone else and that you were never able to see
before. They tell you that this mountain was
once under an ocean and that the next hill
was once a fiery volcano. It's kind of like a
road map, telling you the past.

David's Resume

When you apply for a job in any field, you will need a resume. Here's just part of David's long and impressive resume.

David L. Snyder
Senior Engineering Geologist

EDUCATION
Graduate Studies, Geology, California State University, Northridge, 1987
B.S., Geology, California Lutheran University, 1984

REGISTRATION
California Registered Geologist #5613
California Certified Engineering Geologist #1898
Registered Environmental Assessor #05926
Licensed General Engineering Contractor #679108 (Corporate License)

PROFESSIONAL EXPERIENCE
- Recipient of three grant awards to study earthquake hazards
- Ten years' professional experience
- More than 75 Alquist-Priolo fault studies
- Experienced project manager and supervisor
- Published authority on California faulting
- Consultant to The National Science Foundation and U.S. Geological Survey

AREAS OF SPECIALIZATION
- Geotechnical Risk Assessment
- Downhole logging of landslides
- Paleoseismology
- Residential Distress Causation Studies

Success Stories

Herbert Hoover

Herbert Hoover was a geologist, an engineer, a businessman, and a politician. While attending Stanford University, Hoover worked part-time in the geology department and conducted geological work during the summer. Hoover used his knowledge of geology to become a successful mining engineer. He worked all over the world managing and reorganizing mines and eventually opened his own engineering firm. Hoover was a very successful engineer and soon became a millionaire. His political career began during World War I when he helped people in Europe procure food. He went on to become the head of the United States Food Administration. Later on, this geologist became the thirty-first president of the United States.

Charles Richter

Charles Richter, a seismologist, developed the Richter Magnitude Scale that measures the intensity, or magnitude, of earthquakes. The scale was developed to determine the difference between large and small earthquakes. It is based on a logarithmic scale, which means that a magnitude 8 earthquake has 10 times more ground movement than a magnitude 7, and 100 times more movement than a magnitude 6. After developing the scale, he devoted his career to the study of earthquakes.

Find Out More

You and a career in geology

Geologists piece together parts of history to learn more about the earth. They also conduct experiments that help to explain what is happening to the earth today. This requires patience and perseverance. Let's see if you have the same interests as successful geologists.

1. I am very interested in science, especially earth science.
2. I am patient and pay close attention to detail.
3. I am good at using computers, and I like to use them.
4. I like to travel.
5. I am interested in different types of rocks and how they are structured.
6. I like nature and am interested in protecting it.
7. I like the outdoors.
8. I have often wondered how the earth was formed and how events like earthquakes have changed it.
9. I am good at analyzing things.
10. I like to be challenged intellectually.

Find out more about being a geologist

If you have always liked hunting for rocks, a career in geology may be right for you! For more information about geologists you might want to contact these places:

American Geological Institute
4220 King Street
Alexandria, VA 22302-1507

Geological Society of America
P.O. Box 9140
3300 Penrose Place
Boulder, CO 80301

American Association of
      Petroleum Geologists
Communications Department
P.O. Box 979
Tulsa, OK 74101

CAREERS IN PHYSICS

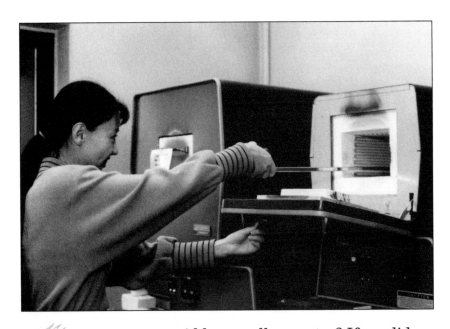

H ave you ever ridden a rollercoaster? If so, did
you realize you were experiencing many of the
laws of physics in action? Gravity and momen-
tum, two of the forces that allow a rollercoaster to work,
are just some of the effects physicists study. Physics is
in every part of our lives; it is the study of energy and
matter. Physicists study everything from atoms to the
stars. The world and the universe are their laboratories

as they try to discover the laws of nature and apply them to everyday life.

What it's like to be a physicist

Most physicists are involved in research and development. As a physicist you will do either applied or basic research. Physicists who do basic research try to increase scientific knowledge, while physicists involved in applied research build on existing discoveries to make new devices and develop new products.

There are two main divisions in the field of physics. Mechanics is the study of motion, and statics is the study of matter at rest. You may decide to specialize in a subfield of physics in one of these areas. As your career progresses, you will be able to switch from one subfield to another because many specialties overlap. Or you may choose to work in a combined field like biophysics, chemical physics, or geophysics.

Let's find out what happens on the job

As a physicist, you could be working for an industry, the government, or a college. Wherever you work, most of your time will be spent doing research. This research can be divided into two categories: experimental and theoretical. As a theoretical physicist you will be trying to determine the laws of matter and energy and attempting to express these laws mathematically. As an experimental physicist, you will be conducting experiments on energy and matter and their interactions. To do your research, you will be using computers, lasers, cyclotrons, telescopes, mass spectrometers, and other equipment.

The pleasures and pressures of the job

One of the greatest joys for scientists is knowing that their research has benefited the world. Discoveries in physics have led to new tools and devices that have done everything from curing the sick to helping clean the air. Fortunately, physics is a field where there are few unusual hazards. If you ever test hazardous materials, strict safety guidelines have to be followed. Most of your time as a physicist will be spent in a laboratory or office. However, at times you may have to work away from home if your research requires large specialized equipment such as a particle accelerator. Although physicists work regular hours, you may find yourself working long and irregular hours when you become deeply involved in research.

The rewards, the pay, and the perks

Physics has been one of the premier sciences throughout this century. Many developments, such as lasers and microchips, have placed physics in the limelight. As a physicist, you would receive the respect and admiration of your community.

The starting salary of a physicist ranges from $30,000 to $41,000.

Those with more education tend to start on the higher end of the salary range. The average salary of a physicist is between $43,000 and $65,000. Physicists working in industry tend to earn the most.

Getting started

For a career in physics, you will definitely need to get a college degree. Most physicists find it necessary to get advanced degrees. Many even begin working on their doctorate immediately after getting their bachelor's degree. To get a Ph.D. you will probably have to conduct some original research. To prepare for college take as many math and physics classes as you can in high school.

Your college placement bureau can help you get interviews for jobs and provide you with solid information about the positions available. If you want to work for the federal government, you will need to take a civil service test.

Climbing the career ladder

When you first get a job in the field of physics, you will probably find yourself doing routine work under the close supervision of more experienced scientists. As you gain experience, you will be given more independence, more complex tasks, and your salary will probably increase. A bachelor's degree will allow you to work as a technician or laboratory assistant. With a master's degree you may be able to do some applied research for private industry. You will need a Ph.D., however, to teach in a 4-year university. In a college or university you can advance from instructor to full professor.

Now decide if being a physicist is right for you

How interested are you in conducting research and developing new products? Do you want to be involved in the continuing pursuit of knowledge about our world? Physicists today are constantly making new discoveries and improving technology. Integrated circuits, used in computers, evolved from physicists' research in solid-state physics.

To become a physicist you will need imagination and an inquisitive mind. You will also need good math and computer skills. Physics can be an exciting, but challenging field. Are you ready to take the challenge?

Things you can do to get a head start

Join your school's science club to start learning more about a career in physics. These clubs usually have scientists as guest speakers who will give you a close look at what it's like to be a scientist. If your school doesn't have a club, you might want to start one. There are also science competitions for high school and college students., Imagine being able to go to the Physics Olympics! For basic information about the field of physics, talk to your science teachers.

$\mathscr{L}et's\ \mathscr{M}eet...$

$\mathscr{X}an\ \mathscr{A}lexander$
$\mathscr{P}hysicist$

As part of her job as a physicist, Xan has given demonstrations on super-conductivity to Congressional committees and helped Senator Al Gore write legislation on environmental and other scientific issues.

What special skills do you need to be a physicist?

If you decide to become a theoretical physicist, you need to be very math oriented. If you want to be an experimental physicist like I am, you should like to tinker and build things.

Tell me about your first job.

I worked on Al Gore's personal staff as a legislative assistant. He was the junior senator from Tennessee at that time. I read proposed legislation on energy, environmental issues, civilian use of space, and scientific policy in order to tell him what the impact would be on Tennessee and the United States. I used my background in science to make recommendations on votes and help him write legislation.

What is your current job?

Right now I have a very exciting job as program manager for the Department of Defense Advanced

Research Projects Agency (ARPA). I am supposed to find high-risk research projects for next-generation electronics that will pay off in research and development and revolutionize the world. I actually handle $25 million to select and fund research for the government. ARPA is the organization that funded the creation of the stealth bomber and the computer mouse.

How did you get your present job?

Networking was the secret. The summer between undergraduate and graduate school, I worked at Bell Labs as part of a fellowship to encourage women to become scientists. Later on, one of my coworkers went to work with ARPA and recruited me for my present job.

Describe a typical day at work.

I spend a lot of time on the phone talking to those who do research for me at schools, businesses, and laboratories all over the country. Much time is spent in the literally millions of meetings I have to attend every day. Time must also be spent reviewing proposals for project funding. I have to pick the new ideas that will be researched and be sure the projects get the needed money. In addition, I need to make sure that all the researchers are talking to each other.

Do you work with many people now?

My job is people intensive and interactive. When I worked in the laboratory, my job was often very solitary.

Xan and Superconductivity in Congress

In 1986, while Xan was working for the Congressional Office of Technology Assessment, a scientific breakthrough occurred: Superconductivity was achieved easily at a warmer temperature. Superconductivity is the complete disappearance of electrical resistance in a substance. Xan's job was to study superconductivity so that she could tell Congress in plain terms what laws needed to be made to handle this discovery as well as what type of superconductivity programs Congress should support.

One day she had to give a demonstration to senators and representatives of how superconductivity worked. When she performed the demonstration, the Congresspeople were so fascinated to see the semiconductor floating above a magnet that they had fun poking at it. Senator Ted Kennedy kept trying to get the members to stop playing and get back to work. You never know what you'll be doing when you choose a career in physics.

Let's Meet...

Tim Childs
Physicist

Tim opted out of a professional football career in order to attend graduate school. He now owns an advanced semiconductor and research company.

What first attracted you to a career in physics?

I was a curious child who always wanted to know how and why things worked. I drove my family mad with my experimenting as I tried to fix mechanical and electrical things and mixed different materials in the sink. So in a way, I was a physicist even as a child because what physicists try to do is figure out what matter is.

Tell me how you got started in your career.

When I was an undergraduate at Florida A & M, I tutored and was a laboratory assistant in physics during the school year. In the summer, I was fortunate to have the opportunity to work on experiments at Bell Laboratories. I studied the properties of solid-state materials, which are metals and semiconductors. This was good preparation for my career because I have always worked with semiconductors.

Did you need any special schooling or training?

Because I have worked in research and development throughout my career, I needed to have a doctorate in physics. I also have a bachelor's degree in physics with minors in math, chemistry, and computer science and a master's degree in physics.

What do you see yourself doing 5 years from now?

For 5 years, I've been running my own company. I have had to spend considerable time working on the business side because that is the area that causes most companies to fail. Five years from now, I would like to be working more on the technical side because that's the work I prefer to do.

What advice would you give young people starting out in physics?

To get a job today, you need to have a broad base of experience. Don't get caught up being isolated in a lab just doing research. Make sure you understand the applications of physics, and be sure to get as much business experience as possible.

Describe your happiest moments on the job.

My happiest moments occur when I see projects come together and see the employees gel as a team. Making some money in my business also makes me happy.

Tim's Career from Research Scientist to Company Owner

After receiving a doctorate in physics, Tim worked as a research scientist at Honeywell in the advanced microelectronics division. It was exciting work because they were developing some of the world's first and fastest semiconductors. Tim soon saw that their research was not being made available fast enough by the company; in fact, it was turning up as products made by other companies. The company let Tim take the technology and make it available commercially.

Tim found it extremely difficult to start a company. His biggest problem was cash flow. He had to move from doing research to commercial application. Tim did everything from selling the product, writing research proposals, to doing accounting.

After the company had been around for a couple of years, more companies started to do business with him. Last year, things really turned around, and today the company has 15 employees. Who knows how big it will get in the years to come.

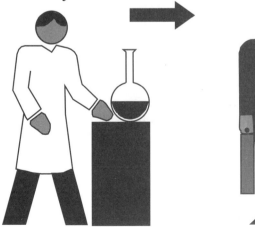

Success Stories

Sally Ride

Sally Ride was the first American woman astronaut to travel in space! In 1983, she was a member of the crew of the Challenger shuttle that went on a 6-day flight in space. During that flight, she conducted experiments and tested equipment. Using a remote-controlled arm, Ride released a satellite into space and then later caught it. Ride received a Ph.D. in physics and then became an astronaut candidate. She has flown in two space missions. Ride has also worked for International Security and Arms Control. She is now a professor of physics at the University of California at San Diego.

Albert Einstein

Albert Einstein is one of the most famous physicists of all time. His many contributions helped bring the world into the nuclear age. By the age of 26, Einstein had already developed the theory of relativity. This theory expressed the equivalence of mass and energy, $E=mc^2$. Although this is probably Einstein's best-known theory, it was his work with light-quanta that won him a Nobel Prize in 1921. The quanta theory prepared the way for the invention of television. Outside of physics, Einstein was a champion of the politically and economically oppressed.

Find Out More

You and a career in physics

Take the following quiz to test your knowledge of physics.

- What causes lightning?
- What keeps you in a roller coaster?
- How fast does light travel?
- What is the definition of mass?
- What is matter?
- Can energy be destroyed or disappear?
- What is the coldest it can get?
- What is fusion?
- What are X-rays?
- What is one fundamental law of nature?
- What is a laser?
- What are the differences among solids, liquids, and gases?
- Why do rainbows form?

If you have often wondered about similar questions or know the answers to some of these questions, then you should consider a career in physics.

Find out more about becoming a physicist

If you would like to become a physicist or are considering a career in the sciences, you might want to contact the following sources for more information:

American Institute of Physics
One Physics Ellipse
College Park, MD 20740

Scientists Institute for Public
    Information
355 Lexington Avenue
16th Floor
New York, NY 10017

Mathematical Association of
    America
1529 Eighteenth Street, NW
Washington, DC 20036

CAREERS
IN
METEOROLOGY

If you are a cloud watcher, you have probably noticed the many different types of clouds that form. Some clouds bring rain or snow, and some spawn violent storms, such as tornadoes. Clouds are just one part of the dynamic atmosphere—the air that covers the earth. And meteorology is the study of the atmosphere. Meteorologists do not just forecast the weather. They also conduct important research that has been applied to air pollution control, air and sea transportation, and trends in the earth's climate.

What it's like to be a meteor- ologist

Meteorologists work all over the country in remote areas as well as in big cities. They are television and radio weather forecasters, researchers, teachers, consul- tants, and technicians. As a meteorologist, you will be working with radar (radio detection and ranging), satellites, computers, weather balloons, and maybe even special aircraft. You'll use these tools to collect and analyze data. And you will often make mathematical models to represent the atmosphere. The results you get from these models can be used to forecast the weather. They also can be used in other areas, like determining the threat of global warming or making airplane flights safer.

Let's find out what happens on the job

If you become an operational mete- orologist, which is the largest group of meteorologists, you will study the temperature, air pres- sure, wind velocity, and humidity to make weather forecasts. You could find yourself working alone in a small weather office or as part of a team in a larger one. Some meteorologists engage in research. If you become a physical meteorolo- gist, you will study areas like the atmosphere's chemical properties and the transfer of energy within it. If you decide to be a climatolo- gist, you will collect, analyze, and interpret past records of rainfall, sunshine, temperature, and wind in specific areas or regions.

Millions of people rely on meteorologists to give them an accurate forecast of the weather every day. Thousands of others depend on meteorologists for their safety (think of a meteorologist working at an airport). In this job you will have the satisfaction of knowing that the work you do affects many people. At the same time, you will have the pressure to make accurate forecasts and meet forecast deadlines. Furthermore, as weather stations operate around the clock to bring people the weather, you may have to work different shifts as well as holidays, unless you are a physical meteorologist working normal hours in an office.

The pleasures and pressures of the job

You will have the reward of knowing that the work you do as a meteorologist could save many lives. Meteorologists give warnings for violent storms and are developing even better storm prediction and detection systems. The warnings they issue allow people to prepare for an impending disaster.

The average salary of a meteorologist is about $48,000, but the salary range is anywhere from $20,000 to $100,000! The beginning average salary ranges from $22,000 to $37,000. The amount

The rewards, the pay, and the perks

you earn will depend on your level of education, your level of experience, and your abilities.

Getting started

To obtain a job in meteorology, you will need a bachelor's degree in meteorology or a closely related field. The federal government is the largest employer of meteorologists. The government requires you to have at least 20 hours in meteorology courses, with at least six of those hours spent in weather analysis and forecasting and another six in dynamic meteorology. Physics and calculus are also required. Choosing the right college is important because only a small number of colleges and universities offer a degree in meteorology; however, many schools offer degrees in related sciences. Before enrolling, be sure you can get the courses you need.

Climbing the career ladder

When you begin your career as a meteorologist, you will probably be doing routine data collection and some basic forecasting. If you work for the federal government, you will most likely start as an intern and advance from there. As an intern you will receive necessary training and experience. If you want to do research on your own, you will need a graduate degree. The more education you have, the greater your chances for advancement will be. As you gain experience, you may be promoted to more complex forecasting jobs or even administrative or supervisory jobs. You could also open your own consulting service.

Now decide if meteorology is right for you

Think about all the meteorologists you have seen on television or heard on the radio. Would you like to do their job? A great way to see how much you like meteorology is to get a part-time job or internship at a local weather station. You would be working with meteorologists and getting a feel for their work. You would also be able to see the research required to determine the weather and the consequences your decisions can have on others' lives. Such an experience would help you quickly discover if you truly want to be a meteorologist.

Things you can do to get a head start

In all fields of science, including meteorology, it is important to get a broad background in the basic sciences while you are still in high school. It is especially important for you to take mathematics and computer science because meteorologists are dependent upon mathematical models and computers for their research. Knowledge of a foreign language would be helpful, too, because it would enable you to keep up-to-date with scientific developments around the world.

Let's Meet...

Mary Newton
Meteorologist

Mary started her career as an operational meteorologist forecasting the weather. She is now an executive officer at the Office of Meteorology of the National Weather Service.

What first attracted you to a career in meteorology?

I was first attracted to meteorology through my love of math and science and an interest in what causes thunderstorms, lightning, hurricanes, tornadoes, and other severe weather. Being a math major, I was also interested in pursuing a graduate degree in a field where I could apply all the principles of math and science learned in my undergraduate training.

Do you use the knowledge/skills you learned in school on the job?

Definitely, yes! You learn how to forecast the weather in school and on the job you apply those "how to" principles to real, live weather events. You build on the forecast principles taught in school with the experience of forecasting for a particular area and before you know it, you have gained considerable expertise in forecasting.

What do you like most about your job?

I like being able to give warnings to the general public that will save lives if (1) the warning is issued in a sufficient length of time for the public to prepare and (2) if the public adheres to the warning.

What do you like least about your job?

Operational forecasting and monitoring the weather involves having someone on the job 24 hours a day, 7 days a week, 365 days a year. So my job does involve shift work. This is one of its disadvantages.

How did you know you would enjoy working as a meteorologist?

The study of weather is an interesting phenomenon. It always changes from day to day. I had an interest in what caused the weather to change, when it would change, and how far into the future we could predict the change. All these elements piqued my curiosity, and I figured I would enjoy working in an environment in which I could answer the question: What is the weather going to be today?

What special skills do you need to be a good meteorologist?

To be a good meteorologist, you must first of all be a good scientist. You must also communicate well, both orally and through writing, and you must have an extreme love for the science.

Mary's Typical Day as an Operational Meteorologist

When Mary got her first job as an operational meteorologist, a typical day at work involved first looking
over past weather to see what had occurred in a particular region during the last 24 hours. She found out
what caused the weather, where the unstable air
masses were located and, if any severe weather had
occurred, if it had caused any fatalities or property
damage. Then she looked at the current weather in
that same region to see if the system that caused yes-
terday's weather had changed. Next, she looked at the
forecast models to see how they were handling the
system and adjusted the models, if necessary, to
develop a forecast that she felt was reasonable. The
forecast was made for precipitation, cloud cover, temperature, and humidity for today, tonight, and
tomorrow. An extended outlook for the next 3 to 5 days
was also made.

Let's Meet...

Steve Zubrick
Meteorologist

Steve works at the National Weather Service as a forecaster and especially likes this career because one day is never the same as another.

Is a career in meteorology something you always dreamed of?

I wanted a career where things always changed. I like variety. Each day, the weather is always different—unlike the day before. Meteorology was a career that seemed to offer variety.

What first attracted you to a career in meteorology?

While growing up in the Midwest, I was always interested in the different kinds of weather that occurred. In winter, we occasionally got a snowstorm. In summer, the frequent thunderstorms fascinated me. I wanted to know why we experienced so many different kinds of weather.

What schooling or training do you need to become a meteorologist?

To be a meteorologist you should attend a college or university that offers a bachelor's degree in meteorology. The U.S. military services also provide training to enlisted personnel who have an interest in weather. Meteorologists need good math, science, and computer skills.

Describe your work environment.

My office is located out in the country near an airport. Inside the office, we have an open area where our forecasters work that is literally surrounded by a ring of computer workstations. These workstations can instantly call up any weather data and images that the forecaster wants to look at.

Do you like to work alone or as part of a team?

The nice thing about meteorology is you get to work both alone and as part of a team. You can spend considerable time by yourself looking at weather maps on a computer, but another forecaster is always nearby so you can talk to each other.

Describe one of your happiest moments on the job.

We had just received and had begun to use data from a new state-of-the-art Doppler radar. This radar has the ability to literally "see" inside severe thunderstorms and determine if the storm has a circulation that can result in a tornado. One day, I was using the radar and saw a circulation indicating a tornado. We issued a tornado warning. A tornado did occur, and the people said they had heard the warning and took cover before the tornado demolished their house.

A Typical Day for Steve

Weather occurs around the clock, 7 days a week. Sometimes you may start your work day at midnight! After getting a weather briefing from the forecaster you relieve, you begin by looking at animated sequences on a computer screen filled with lots of weather data, such as radar, satellite, and surface data. You examine many specialized weather maps that show weather prediction models of how the atmosphere will change during the next several days. After looking at all this data, you discuss what the forecast will be with others at the National Weather Service. Then you either type the forecast or use a special computer program to produce the actual weather forecast that goes to both the public and the media. However, you continue to monitor the weather for any changes or indications of hazardous weather to keep the forecast current.

Success Stories

Evangelista Torricelli

The scientific inventions of this pupil of Galileo provided the basis for meteorology. Torricelli inverted a tube of mercury into another dish of mercury and made a vacuum. The level of mercury in the tube fell when he up-ended it but did not equal the level of mercury in the dish. The space remaining in the tube above the mercury was the first man-made vacuum. Torricelli noticed that the height of mercury in the tube varied over several days. He attributed this change in height to changes in the weight of the atmosphere. Torricelli had invented the first barometer, an important tool in weather forecasting and research.

Radar

Radio detecting and ranging, or Radar, was invented by Sir Robert Watson-Watt in the 1930s. Radar works by emitting radio waves that reflect off an object. The amount of time it takes the waves to return to the sender allows the operator to determine how far away the object is. Radar was very important in World War II. It allowed enemy airplanes to be detected both at night and during the day in any type of weather. This provided time for a warning to be given about oncoming planes. Today meteorologists use this important tool to spot incoming storms.

Find Out More

You and a career in meteorology

Study the following questions:

Why do we have weather?

Why do we have seasons?

Why can't we predict the weather for long periods of time?

How does weather affect me in my everyday life?

How can the study of the atmosphere be used to help people?

If you have ever wondered about any of these questions, you are not alone. Many meteorologists have asked the same questions. Read the next list to see if you have other traits that most meteorologists share.

I like to watch clouds.

I would like to help people.

I am a curious person.

I work well under pressure.

I am worried about air pollution and the greenhouse effect.

I am flexible.

I can work well either alone or in a team.

I like science and math.

I am interested in thunderstorms.

I like to work with computers.

I am interested in using sophisticated tools for research.

I like to do research.

Find out more about being a meteor-ologist

You can learn more about a career as a meteorologist by writing to the following organizations:

National Weather Service
Personnel Branch
1335 East West Highway, SSMC1
Silver Spring, MD 20910

American Meteorological Society
45 Beacon Street
Boston, MA 02108-3693

Association of American Weather
    Observers
P.O. Box 455
Belvedere, IL 61008

National Weather Association
4400 Stamp Road, Room 404
Temple Hills, MD 20748

CAREERS

IN

CHEMISTRY

L ook at the world around you. Everything you see—whether part of nature or made by people—is composed of chemicals. Trees, grass, and sand are chemicals, so are paints, drugs, and electronic components. There are two faces to chemicals: some help cure harmful diseases, while others pollute the environment. Chemistry is the science of these chemicals; it is the study of matter. A career in chemistry offers many different job possibilities. You could work for a police department solving crimes or for a high-technology industry creating new products.

What it's like to be a chemist

While chemists study all aspects of matter, many choose to specialize in one of these fields: organic, inorganic, physical, analytical, and biochemical. If you become an organic chemist, you will study compounds that contain carbon, usually from animal or vegetable matter. As an inorganic chemist, you will study noncarbon compounds, which include metals and minerals. If you are very good in mathematics, you can become a physical chemist. Physical chemists describe many of the physical properties of matter in mathematical terms. Choose a career as an analytical chemist, and you will determine the structure, composition, and nature of substances and be able to test different compounds for purity and quality. Work as a biochemist, and you'll be merging the fields of biology and chemistry as you study the chemistry of living organisms.

Let's find out what happens on the job

Chemists work as teachers, writers, consultants, and much, much more. However, most chemists are involved in some type of research and development. At the research stage, you'll work with ideas for new or modified products, drugs, and materials. During development you will test the products to see whether they can be produced at a reasonable price on a large scale. If the products pass all of their tests, they enter the production stage—the point at which you will prepare them for commercial use.

The pleasures and pressures of the job

Some of the greatest rewards of a career in chemistry can come from inventing a new product or being the first to figure out the composition of a compound. In this job, you'll be able to work most of the time in either a laboratory or an office and typically work regular hours, unless you have an experiment going and have to work long hours and weekends. Certain research projects may require you to work with hazardous materials, but if you follow all of the safety guidelines, you will face little risk of being harmed.

The rewards, the pay, and the perks

Chemists tend to be very versatile; you will probably be able to find a job even when the economy is not doing well. There is a continuing demand for things like new drugs and personal care products as well as specialty chemicals for specific problems or applications.

Beginning salaries in chemistry can range from $24,000 if you have a bachelor's degree to $48,000 if you have a Ph.D. Average salaries range from $44,000 to $65,000 for all levels of education. However, ten percent of all chemists with Ph.D. degrees earn more than $100,000. The more education you have, the better your earning potential will be.

Getting started

For a career in chemistry, a bachelor's degree is usually the minimum requirement. You should choose a college with an undergraduate program in chemistry. But don't just concentrate on chemistry; research and development chemists are increasingly being expected to work on teams where a knowledge of business and marketing is needed.

You can get a head start on gaining experience in chemistry by participating in an intern or co-op program while you are in college. It will be helpful if you start getting a broad science background early in your education. In high school you should take mathematics, physics, chemistry, and life science courses. And be sure to get as much computer experience as possible; it will be invaluable during your career because computers have become an everyday tool for chemists. Studying a foreign language is also recommended for future chemists, especially German, French, or Russian.

Climbing the career ladder

When you first graduate from college, depending upon where you work, you may enter a training program. With a bachelor's degree you will be able to work as a laboratory assistant and maybe even in some research positions testing and analyzing products. Getting a Ph.D. will increase your chances for climbing the career ladder; you will be eligible to do basic research or teach at a college or university.

Now decide if chemistry is right for you

Do you ever wonder how things are made and what holds them together? How can certain chemicals, like water, change from a solid state to a liquid one? Chemistry answers all of these questions. If you are good at working with your hands and like doing experiments, a career in chemistry may be right for you. You will be choosing a career that has many practical applications for everyday life. For example, many synthetic fibers like rubber were developed by chemists.

Things you can do to get a head start

One of the best ways to get a head start in chemistry is to get as much experience now as possible. You could volunteer to help a science teacher or work as a laboratory assistant. Joining a science club at your school and taking part in science fairs are great ways to gain experience in science.

Let's Meet...

John Mitchell
Chemist

John is a research chemist in a national laboratory. While most of his research is conducted on the experimental side of chemistry, he also loves the theoretical side.

What special skills do you need to be a good chemist?

Like all scientists, chemists need to be curious and interested in discovering the reasons behind natural phenomena and how to control them. A chemist also has to be meticulous in his work; small errors in measurements accumulate quickly in a synthesis or analysis, resulting in irrepro- ducible results. Unless we can reproduce a result, it is useless scientifically.

What do you like most about your job?

My research work has a lot of variety. I can be involved in a number of projects at any given time, collaborating with chemists, physicists, and others on compli- cated problems that no individual could hope to tackle successfully. In addition, I derive a lot of satis- faction from achieving the goal of a scientific project, while recognizing that in finding the "answer" I always end up with more questions to explore.

Describe your work environment.

A national laboratory is a big place where many scientists work on many different projects. In my research group there is a strong spirit of collaboration; we all work together to use the talents of each individual for each part of a given project. There is a lot of autonomy in my workplace; no one is watching over your shoulder. Of course, with this freedom comes responsibility; I and other scientists in my group are keenly aware that in order for the group to succeed, each individual must do his or her part proficiently and energetically.

What do you see yourself doing 5 years from now?

I hope to be primarily involved with bench-top chemistry. While most scientists take on increasingly more managerial responsibilities with time, even managers can still do some science. Research is where the fun of discovery is, and that's what brought me into this career in the first place. So, while I will probably be involved in management to some degree, I see myself primarily staying in the laboratory.

What advice would you give young people starting out in chemistry?

Give a lot of thought to what you plan to do with your degree. While advanced degrees definitely improve your chances for a higher-paying, more prestigious position, what you get that degree in is of increasing importance.

John's Career Path

John is a solid-state chemist, which means that instead of stirring up chemicals in beakers and flasks, he heats powders and metals to red hot (and higher!) temperatures to see what new materials form.

John first became interested in chemistry as a high school student. He went off to college knowing he would become a chemist. John applied to graduate school sure that he wanted to be a theoretician. Then, as luck would have it, he took a solid-state chemistry course in the spring of his senior year. It was a turning point. He could see how theoretical leanings could mesh with experimental work in solid-state chemistry. His thesis advisor knew some scientists at Argonne National Laboratory who were doing experimental research on some of the same areas John was studying theoretically. He began to collaborate with them, and a couple of years later he was offered a job at Argonne—as an experimentalist!

Let's Meet...

Claudia Vichland
Chemist

Claudia has worked in a variety of chemistry-related jobs. She now works in the technical service department of a chemistry company as a biochemist.

What first attracted you to a career in chemistry?

I still remember, as a very little girl, going to the lab with my mother who was a research chemist at the time. She set out beakers and safe things for me to work with while she checked on her projects. When I was old enough, I got a chemistry set and even put on a chemistry magic show.

Do you use the knowledge/skills you learned in school on the job?

Oh, yes, all the time! I admit that I can't remember the last time I needed to know the year a certain battle was fought, but all those English grammar rules have really paid off! Knowing how to write essays and spell correctly helped me with writing a chemistry textbook, and I do a lot of editing of other people's work these days. The lab skills from high school were the basic ones that every chemist uses all the time, and the college labs taught me a lot about how to help other people do their jobs.

What special skills do you need to be a good technical service chemist?

When someone asks for help, you must listen carefully to figure out exactly what the caller wants to know and sometimes why he or she is asking. The next skill is making your answer clear and simple enough that your caller understands just what you mean. Patience is important; being able to speak very precise English is critical. Experience in a chemistry lab helps me understand what a caller is trying to do so I can explain techniques better.

What do you like least about your job?

The better our group does our job, the more often customers call back. This makes more and more work for us! There never seems to be enough time in a day to catch up. When something is wrong with a product, some customers can be really rude and difficult to please.

Did you need any special schooling or training?

Chemistry is really a "central science" for many different jobs; it just depends on what direction you want to take. A graduate degree is necessary for special jobs, like teaching. After I earned a bachelor of science degree, I continued in graduate school and earned a master's degree and teaching credentials in mathematics and chemistry. Both of these degrees gave me some additional job choices.

Claudia's Favorite Questions

Claudia is a biochemist for a chemical company with an unusual department: technical service. Customers ask her questions through letters, faxes, and telephone calls from all over the world, about the products the company sells. Two of her most interesting questions are:

"Do you have a recipe for making slime?" (Claudia had one. Now others in her group call Claudia the "slime lady"!)

"Quick! I need a blood detection test that is very sensitive. We found a body and have two suspects. I have 24 hours to prove that the stains on the car seat are blood or I'll have to let the suspects go! Do you have any suggestions?" (Claudia gave the police detective a recipe, told him how to use it, and sent the ingredients by Federal Express!)

Success Stories

Marie Curie

Marie Curie was the first woman to win a Nobel Prize, and she won two! Marie and her husband Pierre, along with another scientist, Henri Becquerel, won a Nobel Prize for the discovery of radiation. While doing research for her thesis, Marie noticed that uranium pitchblende emitted more radiation than was expected. From this observation the Curies went on to separate two new radiating elements—polonium and radium. Her second Nobel Prize was for isolating pure radium and studying its chemical properties. Marie was a woman of many firsts. She was also the first woman lecturer at the Sorbonne University in Paris.

Linus Pauling

Linus Pauling was also a double Nobel Prize winner! Pauling concentrated his research on the nature of chemical bonds. He found that the structure of complex molecules depended on the way atoms were linked. His book *The Nature of the Chemical Bond* is one of the most significant scientific books of this century. Pauling was also very concerned with nuclear weapons. He submitted a petition to the United Nations signed by more than 11,000 scientists that warned about the dangers of radioactive fallout from testing nuclear weapons. He won a Nobel prize for his efforts.

Find Out More

You and a career in chemistry

A career in chemistry can be both exciting and challenging. Even though a career in science is often very rewarding, not everyone has the personality to become a scientist. Chemistry requires patience, logical thinking, and intense concentration. Do the following statements apply to you? If so, then you have the same traits and interests as successful chemists.

I like both science and mathematics.

I can work with extreme accuracy.

I am curious, inquisitive, and like to experiment.

I like to solve problems.

I can apply high levels of concentration for long periods of time.

I am computer literate.

I am interested in the composition, structure, and reactions of various compounds.

I can work with abstract concepts and am able to do exacting analytical work.

I am dedicated and self-motivated.

I can work without a lot of supervision.

I can think logically.

If most of these statements applied to you, then you may want to consider a career in chemistry.

Find out more about being a chemist

If you are interested in becoming a chemist, you may want to contact some of the following organizations for more information.

American Chemical Society
Career Services
1155 16th Street, NW
Washington, DC 20036

American Institute of Chemists
501 Wythe Street
Alexandria, VA 22314

Chemical Specialties
   Manufacturers Association
1001 Connecticut Avenue, NW
Washington, DC 20036

INDEX